When Our Fathers Return to Us as Birds

Made in Michigan Writers Series

GENERAL EDITORS

Michael Delp, Interlochen Center for the Arts
M. L. Liebler, Wayne State University

A complete listing of the books in this series can be found online at wsupress.wayne.edu.

When Our Fathers Return to Us as Birds

Poems by

Peter Markus

WAYNE STATE UNIVERSITY PRESS
DETROIT

ISBN 978-0-8143-4850-5 (paperback)
ISBN 978-0-8143-4851-2 (e-book)

Library of Congress Control Number: 2020946082

Publication of this book was made possible by a generous gift from The Meijer Foundation.

Cover art ©shutterstock.com/g/ullithemrgvia; vector art ©shutterstock.com/g/Teguh+Mujiono. Cover design by Laura Klynstra.

Wayne State University Press rests on Waawiyaataanong, also referred to as Detroit, the ancestral and contemporary homeland of the Three Fires Confederacy. These sovereign lands were granted by the Ojibwe, Odawa, Potawatomi, and Wyandot Nations, in 1807, through the Treaty of Detroit. Wayne State University Press affirms Indigenous sovereignty and honors all tribes with a connection to Detroit. With our Native neighbors, the press works to advance educational equity and promote a better future for the earth and all people.

Wayne State University Press
Leonard N. Simons Building
4809 Woodward Avenue
Detroit, Michigan 48201-1309

Visit us online at wsupress.wayne.edu

*In memory of my father
and for my mother
who was there for him
through the end*

CONTENTS

What My Father Did Not Have to Say

In his final days my father did not speak
because he could not speak. He did not ask
how the car was running or about the kids
or his grand-dog. He did not ask about work.
He did not look out at the boats on the river
to say there goes a thirty-two-footer, or the lines
on that boat are really fine. He did not say
the water was at its highest in twenty-five years.
If his thin lips moved at all it was only when
I wiped them with a wet washcloth, or put yogurt
on a spoon up to them hoping he would eat.
He did not eat and he did not speak and soon
his breathing slowed until there was nothing.
He'd been slowly dying and now he was dead.
I did not know what to say and so I said little
out loud. I walked down to the river where I thought
maybe I would find something there to tell me
what I was supposed to do now. The loons
sat on the water and dove under when a boat
motored close by. They did not sing. Not right then
at least. Only later at night did they call out to each other,
their voices crisscrossing the river in the April dark.

Look at Those Birds

Whatever words my father might speak
now that he is dead are obvious ones: look
at those birds, he tells me, when the ten swans
beat their wings over my head on their way
to somewhere else, even if it's just the other side
of the river where there isn't so much ice.
Pay attention, he says, when just before dark
the doe and her two fawns cross the road
stopping briefly to look at me as if to say
we see you, we know you live here too.
When I go down to the river. When I walk
through the trees. When I look at the sky.
Father. Father. Father. Bird. Bird. Bird.

The Name of the Father, the Name of the Fish

In the moments after my father died
I lathered up his face with soap to shave him.
It was the very least that I could do after
everything he had always done for us.
My mother praised my tenderness, how close
I was able to get, under his nose and neck,
those places where when he was alive
he would pull his face away and tell me to stop.
Afterwards, I went down to the river to draw
a glass of water from the river we both loved.
I dipped my hands into the water to anoint him,
in the name of the father and the fish. On his head,
his hands, his feet, his belly, upon his heart.
I made the sign of the cross, followed by a fish,
next a crescent moon. I raised the glass of water
which sparkled, it was so clear and so clean.
As was my father. As was the clarity that death brings.

Practice

How cruel that for the last years of his life
he could not speak. Could not get out of bed
to walk himself to the bathroom, could not
wipe his face clean, could not shave or shower
or brush his teeth without the help of his wife
or son. And let's not speak about the plastic bag
fixed to the side of his bed, or the rubber hose
that ran to it, draining out what was in his bladder.
The indignity of such reduction, the body as a vehicle
of betrayal. This for a man who for sixty years
rarely took even an aspirin, who never complained,
never missed a single day of work. The doctors
were only human and of little help. When he could speak
he often made the joke about the medical profession:
"That's why they call it practice." They never got it right.
In the end, cause of death: malnutrition. He starved
himself to death. The one thing he had control of.
He turned his head away from the window with a view
of his beloved river and went to sleep. Died on a Sunday.
A beautiful sunny day. Blue skies. Loons on the river.
The river water that his son anointed his body with
clear enough to drink. The way it glistened in the glass.
Everybody amazed at how clean it was. How transparent.

House with No Light Left on Inside It

He misses both his dog and his father
equally. How they stopped eating
on the same day but the dog lasted
a week longer than the father did.
He now walks alone through the trees
with both of them by his side. Talks
to them both in a whispering voice
as morning takes shape out of the dark.
Wishes they were both still with him
though he is grateful for the times together
they had. In the trees there are birds
singing that make him wonder if maybe
both fathers and dogs return to us
as birds. There were loons on the river
the night his father drew his last breath.
There was the eagle all winter long
which he believed to be the dead father
of a fishing buddy. And the crow
his wife saw swoop down from the sky
when she said his father's name.
I would like to come back a sparrow
he thinks as he walks toward the rising sun.
Yes, a sparrow, he thinks, and bows
his head as if in prayer, or else like a bird
bending down to eat the breadcrumbs
that a young boy might leave behind him
in the woods to help find his way back home
to a house with no light left on inside it.

Everything Where I Have Left It

What is so different about this house
when it is dark? Which is how I prefer it.
When there is not so much to see.
The trees outside in shadow. The sky
not so stark and apparent. The mystery
of things unseen even just across this room.
What I know is right here remaining unchanged.
Everything where I have left it. Waiting
to be eventually thrown out. Like the dead.
Like how they came and took away my father
when it was time. When my voice into the phone
told them what had happened. When I said
my father has died. Is dead. How otherwise say it?
How outside it was still light out. How inside
everything had suddenly become so clear.
So certain. Like the water I brought back up
to the house from the river. The weight
of the glass in my hand. Such utter clarity
when I held it up to the light. The way the sun
shined through. And yes, made it sparkle.
What was visible that night aside from the stars.
Not the loons calling out across the river.
Not the heart alone in its own dark house.

I Take a Walk with the Gods

I take a walk with the gods down to the river
to see if we might reach an agreement. I see
their rowboat pulled up onto the shore, waiting.
The moon above the steel mill's smokestacks
watches us, not like an eye, but like the moon.
They are dressed like and look like fisherman
without rods or tackle or bait. But they have no
interest in catching fish. The gods have a job
to do. There is no pleasure in their actions.
If anything, like the rest of us, they seem
bored, going through the motions, punching
the clock. For my father, the wait is over.
For them, once they cross the river, it will be
time for lunch. I do not beg for one more day.
Those days are over. Wait here, I tell them.
And walk back up to the house where my father
is in his bed being tended to by my mother.
They are holding hands. My mother is the anchor
to my father's boat. Made of wood, it leaks,
takes on water, will soon sink. My father is a fish
who will swim away once we choose to release him,
his mouth and head shaking twice to let us know
he'll be okay, before disappearing into the dark.

Brothers and Fathers and Sons

We walk in the rain along the levee
in memory of our fathers lost last winter.
Our dogs run up ahead of us in the marsh
looking for something hidden to flush.
Maybe the spirits of our fathers are birds
hunkered down in the brush, waiting
to take flight, giving us one last chance
to see them, to say goodbye, before
disappearing for good over the tree line.
In the distance we hear gunshots.
There are ducks watering in the slough.
We walk heavy with mud and a sorrow
we choose not to talk too much about.
We talk instead of our mothers who live
in houses that are haunted by the absence
of our fathers. Our fathers in the fields
watching us as the day now darkens.
As the dogs cut through the cattails.
As us brothers keep walking in silence.
When the moon appears tonight it will be
waning. Which doesn't mean it is anything less.
Only that some small part of it can't be seen.
Because it isn't lit. But is there in shadow.

Who Walks in the Rain Walks on Water

Listen. I am a river that holds more fish
than I know what to do with. At night
the moon lightens what is otherwise dark.
A boat anchored off the tip of an island.
A few others adrift. Most at the dock
or in hoists until morning. In the rain.
The houses with their porch lights on.
Burning. Some making a hissing sound.
Moths circling as if being summoned home.
At dawn a man and his dog on a walk.
A stone offers itself up from the mud.
He picks it up to skip it. Watches it sink.
Thinks to himself, When I was a boy.
The things he could do with a rock. A river.
Those days when he could see bottom.

The Dark Above the River Is Light

The morning sky that takes shape
above the river is made out of light.
You can't convince me that it's not.
Even when the clouds make it dark.
The light is there waiting to be light.

South of White Rock, Lake Huron, July 1979

We were throwing stones, being boys,
when I dared my cousin, older by two years,
to see if he could hit the seagull perched
out on the big rocks sticking out of the water.
He cocked back his arm as far as it could go
and threw, and we both watched the slate
cut through the summer air like a boomerang
we knew was not coming back. When it hit
the gull in its neck the bird folded in on itself,
falling into the water. We could not believe it.
Death and the rocks seemed so far from shore.
We waited and waded in when the waves washed
the dead bird in close enough for us to reach it.
It was white and limp and lighter than I expected.
Years later, our fathers both dead, I remember
that summer day, when we were young and stupid
kids. Too bad our fathers weren't around to stop us.
We dug a hole deep in the sand, put death down in it.
Then covered it up, never talked about it. Until now.
Strange how birds have a way of taking us back
in time, through the years, wings cutting the wind,
the air, the blue skies above the lake, the silence.

There Is Singing

The bird outside the window
is made of ash. There is no
going home. You are already
there, sheltered from the wind.
Somewhere there is singing.
Elsewhere there is a song.

Last Song

When the priest came to the house
to read my father his last rites
he sang like I imagine a bird might sing
when it too is singing about death.
A nest in a storm blown from a tree.
Eggs on the ground broken. Afterwards
I walked down to the river to see
what I might find there. It was as if
nothing had changed. The buoys
were anchored in their places to mark
where the water dropped off deep.
The steel mill kept its silence. I wanted
to dive in headfirst to see what
my body would do with the cold.
How my heart would be made to race.
What would happen if I stopped
swimming. How long it would take
before I was carried away by the current,
my skin turning numb and blue.

What the Birds Keep Trying to Tell Him

Among the slags of ice on the river
the song of a solitary crow in the trees
above him as he walks with his dog
or his wife and the wind that insists it
is still winter. Walking with the crow's song
ringing in his ear. How he can't not think
about his father dead now how many days.
What these birds keep trying to tell him.
If anything other than look, I am right here.

More Birds Than I Know What to Do With

The bird that flew into the window
was being chased by a bird that did not fly
into the window. The bird that flew
into the window is dead. A broken neck,
I imagine. Who can know the cause
of death other than to say that it flew
into the window. The glass did not break.
If you've ever held a bird in your hand
you already know how light it is, how little
a bird weighs. It's almost nothing.
It's no wonder that a thing so weightless
can fly. Yet when I walked the bird
over to the garbage can and dropped it gently in,
it made a sound. The final note
in its song. A heavier than expected thud
that echoed briefly—it lingered, I was held by it—
like when you hit your hand once on a drum.
Elsewhere, in a tree, some other bird was singing.
Other birds flew into a window we call sky.

I Did What I Could to Keep This

I am here to translate my father's death
into fruit. Something that can be held. To bring
it up to your lips the way I spooned strawberry
yogurt up to his and said to him the word "Eat."
There was no use, in the end. There was no hunger.
When you are eighty-six and stop eating you die.
On his death certificate, under "Cause of Death,"
the word "Malnutrition." I did what I could to keep this
from my mother. When she saw it, I watched her face.
What was left inside her went to someplace else.
I said something to her to make sure she knew
it wasn't her fault. There was nothing she could do.
"It means that he stopped eating" is all I said.
My mother nodded. My father, later, zipped into a bag.
And taken away from us forever. The man who did
the zipping took me by the elbow to tell me we might not
want to watch. I took my mother into the other room.
Then went back because I wanted to see. My mother returned
to see too. They wrapped my father up in a sheet my mother
had recently washed. It smelled of lavender and bleach.
I had shaved my father minutes after he drew his last breath.
Wiped his face clean in a way that pleased my mother.
It was the least I could do. Later, when I asked if she was hungry,
she shook her head to tell me no. I'd slept on the carpeted floor
the night before, my father's last. Kept watch asleep in my clothes
behind the couch beside his bed. If I dreamed I don't remember.
I don't remember more than this little bit I am trying to hold.
This small fruit. A single grape pulled from the cluster in the fridge.
They put my father into a van and headed south along the river.
The road to the bridge gets bumpy was all I told them after
they shut the rear doors where they slid inside the narrow gurney
with my father's dead body on it. He had already started to become
something else. In the darkness at the edge of that road, I stood
for a little while before walking down to the river, where the dark water
moved in its usual ways, as if it were following my father, going under
the bridge they drove across as they took him even further away.

The Old Neighborhood

I think, in the end, my father knew
who I was. That he saw me and would say
my name. That he knew me as his son.
Sometimes, I know, he thought I was one
of the guys from the office, or an old friend
from high school. The old neighborhood
he called it. I think he'd often go back
to that place inside his head. 1032 Rademacher.
Delray. See himself falling in love with the girl
who would later become his wife. My mother.
Who would love him through the end. I don't think
he could ever imagine what that would be like:
to be taken care of, to be dressed and fed, the bed
sheets changed beneath him. To be wiped clean.
To be a child again. To be mothered again. To think
that at times I was his father even. To believe
I would protect him, like any good father would.
That I'd lift him up, into my arms. Carry him home.

Because I Could Not Sing

I am walking along the river's boardwalk
north of the bridge looking into the distance
at Detroit fifteen miles away. It's night
and the blast furnace fires of Zug Island
offer up a rising sun that is as man-made
as the wheeled bodies of steel that we drive
into the city with. I am walking my dog
who is nearly twelve which in dog years
I know is the same age as my father
who is in a bed right now in a living room
across the river unable to sit up or turn
on his side, let alone do what he used
to love to do which was take a simple walk
with my dog or tend to his two boats. I am
like my father in that I too love walking
my dog and taking care of the two boats
that now are mine. Soon, I said to my father
the other day, there'll be boats on the river.
I pointed out the window to the Whaler
on the trailer out back in the backyard.
I don't know that what he was looking at
was boat. There were trees back there
for him to see but only my father knows
what else his eyes were able to name.
After a while I said the words, Your boat.
And he nodded his head as if to say
he got it. In truth I don't know that he did.
In the distance back to the river I can see
the scorched sky above Great Lakes Steel
where my father used to work in the days
before I was even born. A long time ago.
52 years. He made it out of there alive,
walked out after six years of sweating metal.
One of the lucky ones. Got a job wearing
a suit at Ford Motor where twenty-five years
after escaping Great Lakes he dragged
his dropped left foot out of World Headquarters

to spend the rest of his days in the house
on an island in the middle of the Detroit River.
Here again, he'd tell you, one of the lucky ones.
A place on the water. It's what he'd always
wanted. What he dreamed. He pinched pennies
at both home and work. And made it happen.
Now it's all come down to this. No one
could have predicted and no one can prepare
you for how we leave the world. Just like
no one can prepare you for the miracle
of when your own daughter or son enters
the world asking for just one thing: to be loved.
To be cared for. To be held. To teach us
how to love. To think not only of ourselves.
I am walking now in the shoes of my father.
Along a river that I know has two sides to it.
As every story does. This is how I kiss my father
goodbye. This is how I hold his hand and sing.

The Song and the River

The days pile up, one on top
of the other, until we are standing
on top of a mountain looking
out at a sky with no sun or moon.
Not even the stars ask who we are.
Even the sound of our own voice
inside our head belongs to a stranger.
When we try to remember or say
our name we are left with a silence.
When you reach out for the wing
of a passing blackbird it turns away.
Its black eye says to you not yet.
Below there is a crack in the earth
that turns out to be a river. Too deep
to walk across and with a current
too swift to swim, you wait to see
if maybe a boat might take you.
When no boat comes you walk back
home to the bed by the window
with a view of the river. You climb
back into the quiet. Across the river
the tallest point is a smokestack
that no longer belches gray smoke.
Beneath your bed pillow is a stone
you placed in your pocket years ago
during one of your many walks
along the river. Stones are prayers,
are songs only the birds can hear
when they take us up on their backs
to carry us home. Home, my father
likes to say. I want to go home.
You are home, I say. Maybe he sees
the mountain and the blackbird.
Maybe the stranger's voice is his own,
in the silence, singing him home.

My Father's Only Son

As a child, on Detroit's southwest side,
my father and his friends used to run
through alleys and climb on garage roofs
to shoot at each other with BB guns.
Later, my father and his friends—Greeks,
Armenians, Hungarians from Delray
—shot real guns in Korea. Still kids,
they learned how to look tough and grown up
in photographs, squinting at the camera
with cigarettes hanging from their lips.
The truth is they were homesick and scared
to admit it, scribbling letters home to girls
they'd never even kissed, or maybe only once.
I like it when I try to imagine my father
as a kid. As a young man. When he was dying,
he was like a child to me, the way I fed him
oranges, wiping the juice from his chin. At times
he thought I was his father. Or a friend
from the old neighborhood. Maybe some guy
he worked midnights with. But I was just his son,
his only son, and more often than not
I let my father believe whatever he wanted.
I was willing to be whoever might help him remember
all the times he believed he would never die.

On the Island in Search of My Father

I drove around the island looking
for my father. There was little other traffic
because it was night. Saw more deer
than I did people. The lights of the buoys
on the river blinked on and off,
red and green. But it was mostly dark.
Mostly silent. I drove with the windows down
hoping to hear my father's voice
calling from a ditch, or worse: the water.
In my mind I imagined myself able
to save him. My father's Lincoln
stuck in the mud, its silver hood ornament
hidden in the cattails. Or submerged
in the weedy shallows, my father shivering
behind the wheel, holding onto it tight,
thinking this would keep him alive.

I Did Not Hear the Loons Until Later

The bird on the buoy does not need to know
we are watching. Or that across the river
there is a small boat turned over on its side
for the winter. The fish are here with us
even if we don't see them. When the water
makes a sound it is only to remind us perhaps
that it is moving, that sometimes the wind
changes the way we see it. When my father
finally died I did not hear the loons right away.
Only later. When I stood down at the dock
and looked. Then heard them first. Then saw
what was behind that sound. Which wasn't human.
That cry. That calling out. But was the closest
to what I felt when I closed my eyes and decided
in the dark of night that I had seen enough.

A Portrait of My Father at the End as Sisyphus

How frightened my father must have been
not at the end, but closer to what I now see as
the beginning. The walk down the mountain.
Or maybe Sisyphus on his way up. The boulder
so close, his warm face pressed against it,
his hands and shoulders braced to begin
the long journey to the top. Pushing the rock
inch by inch, doing his best not to stop. At the top
stepping aside and having to let go to watch
the giant stone roll back to where he'd started.
The momentary feeling of achievement. The long
walk down the mountain with nothing to show,
nothing to hold, only the dust in his hands.

Where There Is a River There Is a Light

When I went down to the river to draw a glass of water from it
I was really going to the river to let my father go. His spirit.
To release him and it from a body that had already begun to go
cold. Turn stiff. So strange how the living become the dead so quick.
When I walked back up from the river with a glass full of the river,
the water glistened in the sunlight pouring in through the living
room window with its view of the river, the steel mill looming silently
on the river's other side. I dipped my fingers into it and touched my father
on his head, his hands, his feet, his heart. Here I drew an invisible fish,
a moon, a cross, a line to represent our beautiful river. There were loons
out on the river that night singing out across the darkness of the night
after the two men drove up in their van to take my father's body away.
I shaved him one last time before they wrapped him up, my mother happy
to see his face so clean it was almost shining. As if there was some light,
or lighthouse, at the very least a buoy blinking inside him offering us a little
hope, to let those of us left alone on this river know which way was home.

April 6

I am getting the boat ready.
Took off the tarp. Tightened screws.
Filled up both tanks.
The batteries are charging.
Tuesday I will put the Whaler in.
I wish you were here to at least
see and hear me working.
A nod of your head when I'd say
we got her in the water.
Then I'd drop to my knees
to drain your catheter
with the smell of gasoline
still on my hands.

On Turning Fifty-Two

Up early on the morning of my fifty-second birthday.
To read poetry in the dim yellow lamplight of pre-dawn.
My son, about to turn twenty, asleep on the couch.
My wife in our bed sleeping too. Hopefully dreaming.
Of us making a love made strange through its maneuvers.
That it lasts with something resembling fortitude.
The dog licks her own paws to get at something there.
The quiet that hums between my ears. The guitar
across the room with its missing strings wishing I knew
how to play it. Accepting that I don't. At least not much.
Still I pick it up. My fingers make the shape of the familiar.
A silver sound jangles out. I have heard it all before.
Give me instead the muted or even the out of tune.
The not knowing what to name the chord. Dissonance.
Discord. The feedback I remember when I was sixteen.
Standing too close to the amp. Facing it. Not turning away.
How the impulse would be to reach up and touch my ears.
But I never did. Which explains why I often hear myself
saying the words "Say again." I want you to know I care.
That I'm wanting to listen. Even when the past gets in the way.
We carry our mistakes with us into the present forever.
You can go home again but the house is now abandoned,
or torn down, or painted yellow, and the people inside
don't know your name and are indifferent to your story.
The birds go on singing regardless. The new day and year
fill with snow or light or sometimes if we're lucky both.

No Words

If I could get away with it
there'd be no words here at all.
A feather, or the entire wing
of a bird whose beginning
I know was in a nest in a tree
I often stand beside with a hand
reaching out to touch its bark.
A leaf too, a part of a branch,
both of which have fallen as if
to give themselves to this poem.
And fish, maybe just a few
silvery scales that will shimmer
luminescent when we raise
the poem up to the day's failing
light. And let us not forget
the river itself, which cannot
be held, which when we step
into it both of us are never
the same. And what of the sun?
What of the morning's dark?
The moon that floats above us
like a boat with no oars drifting
through the night. Maybe the stars
are actually fish, or the lights
of other boats, or the blank pages
of notebooks held up close to
the candle's flame waiting to be
burned, or hoping to be made
into poems, or feathers, or fathers,
or birds, or trees, fish, or river,
or darkness, the sun that will erase
it all when there are no words,
when there is nothing left to say,
when no words can get it right.

Too Many Days, or Where the River Turns to Lake

It has been three days since he's seen the river.
Three too many days if you ask him. To be inland means
in from the river. There is a river running inside him.
For the past few years he had his father to go see before
walking down to the river. Now he has his mother
he goes to see in her grief. Let's go down to the river
is what he tells her, and he takes her by the arm to safely
walk her down. She watches him fish. She is momentarily
happy, it seems, when he catches something. It's not
what he's fishing for but it's a fish regardless. He throws
what he isn't after back. His mother asks about the hook.
Doesn't it hurt. He makes up what he thinks is possibly true.
That the fish do not feel pain. That they don't have nerves
in their mouths which is where the barbed hook takes hold.
He doesn't know for sure if this is true. He knows that if
a lie is repeated often enough it begins to carry its own truth.
Today the geese are grouping up on the river, preparing
for some migratory trip. They make their loud honking sounds
though his mother does not turn her head to hear them.
She is elsewhere inside her own thoughts, he knows. She is
somewhere, he hopes, with his father, on a boat, perhaps,
like when they were both still young, without kids, with the wind
filling their sails, pushing them out of the river, moving into the lake.

When It Is Dark Enough to See

Out where the river turns into the lake
there is a boat drifting underneath stars.
I want to learn to speak that language
where sky means bird and father and fish.

Still Life in Winter with River Ice and Sky

I am not going to tell you about this cold snap,
the past three days with highs below zero.
If my father were still alive, maybe he'd tell me
about the winters when he was a boy, how
he used to play on the frozen river by Belle Isle,
that it was possible back then to walk across.
Yesterday I stepped out onto the ice and stood
alone facing the steel mill, its long black body
stretched out motionless against a clear blue sky.
How it no longer makes what it was built to do.
That it hasn't had ore inside it since I was a boy
when on Friday nights we'd build a fire in the woods
next to the slag hills and drink whiskey and talk
about not getting laid and our plans for getting out
of this town. It was a dead-end town even then.
But it was a town with a river and even when I left
I knew I'd be coming back. What I didn't know
was that I'd be back in time to watch my father die,
the two of us looking out the living room window
at the river and the mill grown thick with weeds.
They'll never make steel here again. And I'll never
have a father to walk down to this river with,
our breath like smoke rising into the winter sky.

Skin of River and Bone

This is not a river to wade out in. It is not
a river to cross. The bottom, to begin with,
is made of mostly mud. It is not uncommon
to sink down in up to your knees. Not a feeling
you want to know, unless you have to fix
a dock beam damaged by the breakup of ice.
My father was the one who always took care of
what was broken. Until he could no longer.
And handed that hammer down to me. His hands
were big-knuckled and calloused when I was a boy.
It wasn't until I saw them near the end clutching
the bedsheet did I realize how small they'd become.
How big mine had gotten. How I had to learn
to hammer nails into wood. My own flesh tearing.

Walking Out Alone onto the February River

I walk out onto the frozen river thinking
I am alone. But we are never really alone.
Ten swans flying overhead remind me
to always look up. On the ice, I walk out
with a stick to lead the way, to gauge
the thickness, to stand in the cold holding
something. The buoy I know is red
that marks the edge of the channel is buried
with snow and ice. I look up and down
this river thinking I might see another face.
Am glad when I don't. Only river. Only birds.
Only ice and sky and a voice that could only be
my father saying I have gone out far enough.

We Did Not Know the Difference

When I cross the bridge I always head south
along the river before circling back north to go see
my mother. When my father was alive I'd turn
immediately north, the quickest way, the fastest path
into an emergency. Even when he was safe in bed
and not fallen onto the floor I'd drive fast to ward off
that possibility. On a good day he'd take my hand
and shake it and sometimes bring it up to his lips.
Why talk about the bad days, the times he'd grit his teeth
and tell me to get away, or worse: when he'd beg me
to take him with me. Or the nights he'd look at me
as I was leaving and say with his eyes: stay. I struggled
to sit for more than a few minutes on the couch beside his bed.
There were things that needed to get done in this house
on the river with my father dying inside it: light bulbs to change,
dishes to wash, the garbage that needed to be taken out.
Dead batteries in my father's old cars. Tires in need of air.
I busied myself with the things my father used to do. I tinkered
with the boats, the outboard engine. Oiled the gears on the dock.
Tightened nuts and bolts and screws. I wasn't good at doing
such things. But someone had to do it. Or go through the motions,
at least. Truth be told, I went down to the river to get away.
I'd look out across the moving waters at what I could not touch,
the red and green buoys that marked the channel, the steel mill
shipwrecked on the river's other side. I'd gaze down to see
if I might spot a pike cruising lazily through the shallows.
If the light was right I might see one, knifing its long narrow body
through the light green murk. Sometimes only a few minutes
would pass, though turning back to face the house it was as if years
had moved beyond us. I was no longer a young man. My father
was still dying. Night had settled in around us. Everything was suddenly
so still and so quiet it was as if we were all of us already dead.

I Am Tempted to Say I Know Nothing

I am tempted to say I know nothing
of this place, which is mostly true.
Here is the river. There is the lake.
Out further still there is the lighthouse.
Beneath these boots is limestone
once hidden by water. I am learning
the names of birds, but there are still
too many to keep up with and I end up
seeing the same ones over and over
which doesn't bother me. What if all I want
is more of the same? Maybe in the end
that is abundance. A handful of words
to put into a sentence and be able to say it
in a single breath. Goose, swan, duck,
seagull, eagle, loon, blackbird, red-winged,
black-eyed, beaked, boned, feathered.
And for all of it to add up. To make sense.
What else could I ask for? All of this
will be here when we're not, our bones
ground down to a fine white dust.

Winter Birds

Where have the five swans gone?
Birds that all summer had gathered
around the dock. At times hissing
when I would come near, as if to say
you are not allowed here. This river
is our river, they wanted me to know.
Six months to the day my father died.
Perhaps this is coincidence. Or maybe
it is my father's way of reminding me
he is gone. And unlike those birds
that winter elsewhere, that fly south
to open water, he is never coming back.

We Just Wanted to Get Him Home

Twice now the past week a Great Blue Heron
has been down at the end of the dock,
doing or waiting for what I do not know.
Maybe this is just his down time, and eventually
this grand, gangly bird will take to the sky
or the water to look for food. But I also think
that maybe he is waiting for me to see him,
though as soon as I get too near his wings
unfold open as if pulled by a string from above
like the marionette of an airplane
lumbering at liftoff. I stand and watch
as he disappears, long legs trailing behind him,
the summer's blue sky and river below
the kind of place any of us would be lucky
to die in. The last time my father was in the hospital,
I told the doctor: *We just want to get him home.*
I did not have to end this sentence with
to die. Looking back, would it have been any better
for my father to die down at the river's edge,
to trip and fall off the end of the dock, hit his head
against the concrete decking, and drown
in four feet of water? What would be the point
of answering this, my own dumb question?
The heron squawking is a dying language
I do not speak. A bird in flight getting smaller
in the distance and against midday's miraging light
until he is no longer with us in this world.

The Bird Inside My Father's Chest

At the end of his days my father
was becoming transparent. His skin,
I mean, was almost see-through.
It was as if I could look inside his chest
where a bird sat as if on a branch
of a tree waiting to fly. Waiting
to spread his wings.

What I Know Is Not My Father

My father lives now not in a house
but in the river and on this boat beside me
as I cut the engine and drift downriver
past the steel mill and the hospital
where no one has died or walked away
in close to twenty years. So much of what
remains with us is just the husk or skin
of what once was. The urn in my pocket
is mostly just something small for me to hold.
I know it's not my father even though
it is his bones ground down to a fine white ash.
My father is more in the river and sky,
the Great Blue Heron on the rocky shore,
the osprey flying overhead, the seagull on a tree
floating beside us. We know there are fish
in these dark waters even though we cannot
see them. Sometimes when I snag bottom
I am fooled for a moment that it's a fish.
But a fish is alive in your hands the moment
you set the hook. The way it shakes
its head as if to say I'm not going
without a fight. My father held on longer
than he could. In the end he pulled his knees
in up to his stomach and went to sleep.
Eventually his breathing stopped. I was reminded
of when I was a child up north, the first time
I hooked and caught a catfish. Four hours later,
sucking at summer's cruel air, about to be gutted
in the kitchen sink, this fish refused to die.
It flared its boned fins even after I slid the filet knife
inside it. Even after I chopped off its head,
when I tossed what was left of it out into the yard
for the raccoons to eat, I saw its whiskers move,
its black eyes opened wide, staring up from the ground
at a sky that was suddenly radiant with light.

Carrying the Fish

The fish was dead and had been dead
for several days. But the dog sniffed at it
as if making sure. The fish was dead
on the levee road which left me to wonder
how did it get here. Maybe a small boy
fishing with no father could not work
the hook loose. Maybe a bird—an eagle
or osprey—believing he could carry it
back to his nest failed to hold on as it flew.

What Was Never His to Begin With

He carries the tiny silver urn
with his father's ashes in it
in his trouser pocket because
he isn't yet ready to give
his father back to the river.
Perhaps he will never be quite
willing to give his father up.
It will be a selfish gesture
to hold on to what was never
his to begin with. Until then
the urn's cold metal presses up
against his thigh. Holding on
to the chrome wheel of the boat
he heads downriver eyeing
the Great Blue Heron near shore,
its long yellow beak stabbing
at the dark and muddy waters
moving steady in between its legs.

When No One Was Looking I Looked

I have a single photograph of my father
dead. The expression on his face
a perfect sentence. The question mark
of his parched lips. The silence holding on
at the end: steadfast in its discipline.

Man on Boat

Woke up, got out of bed, took a walk.
This is what my father can only dream of.
He dreams of going down to the river
where a boat is waiting anchored to shore.
He rows through the shallows, through weeds.
Then eventually gets to the deeper waters
of the channel. He sits back and lets the current
take him away. He drifts downriver towards the lake.
On the lake the day gradually turns to night.
The stars in the sky are a constellation of fish.
He begins counting but stops at ninety-nine.
Then imagines that he is lost in the woods
where there are more leaves than stars.
He builds a fire to keep away mosquitoes.
When he wakes up again it is morning again.
His hands are fish-scale-covered. It's as if
his skin has been dipped in stars. The moon
in the western sky is barely visible. Like a ghost.
Or like a memory you might only imagine.

What in the Night the Moon Makes

My father walks back to the house in the dark
up from the river singing so I can barely hear it.
What can we possibly know of the darkness
he speaks about, sings about, knows about now
that he is dead? Yes, he is dead but he is walking
in a way that says he refuses to believe this.
Walking up the wooden steps two rungs at a time
as if to show off this strength that he is feeling
in his limbs. For years he could not feel his feet,
his fingers, the nerves running down to them fried.
Now he glides and climbs without having to hold on
to the wooden handrail gone wobbly recently with rot.
Maybe my father's singing has lifted him above this river
where the red buoy that marks the edge of the channel
blinks on and off in the dark. Maybe what I am hearing
is just the wind moving through the trees and what I think
is my father is only a Purple Martin chasing mosquitoes
in the night with the moon making all of this visible.

When the Light Is Still Present but Fading

Each day begins in the dark. Night comes
when the light is still present but fading.
Across the river my father in bed sleeping.
Possibly dreaming. Sometimes talking
to those he counts among the already dead.
His own mother and father. An older sister.
All three of them waiting at the edges of dawn.
He stood above them all in their own beds.
Now they hover near, I imagine, watching.
Maybe even reaching out to touch his hand.
To say it's okay, he'll be coming home soon.
Until then my mother wakes up with the dark.
Already alone. But not prepared for what is
coming. A house on the water. And solitude.
The sound in her ear ticking away the silence.
When daylight rises it is always behind her.
The sun breaking through the trees. The river
slowly becoming bluer than it actually is.

Maybe Next Time

For too many years I told my father
not now, I was too busy, maybe next time.
I had work to do, which was a lie.
He tried to teach me when I was a boy
what to call the parts under the hood
of a car, how to pound a nail, chop wood,
winterize the boats, shoot a free throw.
In other words, how to be a good father.
I struggled to pay attention. I did my best
to hold the light and was usually thinking
about a girl, or a party, or a poem I wanted
to write. I wish I would have listened
to the gods that were screaming in my ear—
the poem's in front of your face. Make use.
Your father one day is going to be dead.
And before he dies he is going to shit the bed.
You and your mother will roll him over
to change the sheets and he will struggle
just to tell you why can't you leave me alone.
On one of his last days I fed him strawberry yogurt.
I spooned it up to his lips. His head was turned away.
A dose of my own medicine. He had better things to do.
Death was a boat waiting on the river's other side.
A poem waiting to be memorized. Waiting to be written.

The Sentence I Am Trying Not to Write

I am sitting in the dark near the window
watching it snow. It is still too early
to know if my mother will call to tell me
my father is dead. For now he is alive
asleep in his bed with a view of the river.
Or maybe he is up early this morning
looking out at the five swans that move
through the watery dark, their long necks
bent like question marks, the silence
of the hour asking, Will today be the day?
Meanwhile the sun rises like a gigantic period
at the end of the sentence I am trying not to write.

Slow Dance with My Father with No Music

I am sitting here in the morning darkness
thinking of you. Father. How you will never read
the poems I have been writing about you
these past fourteen months. What I was seeing
as I watched you die. Watching you live on.
Going to your bedside. Lifting you up into a chair
with wheels to shave you. So that your wife
who is my mother still could change the sheets
on the metal bed with a view looking out at the river.
So I could feed you too. And brush your teeth.
Trim your hair. Little things, yes. Acts that require
patience. And tenderness. And a willingness
to let go when it got to be too much. For a time
you were able enough to walk the few steps
to get back into bed. But even this, after a while,
got to be too much to expect. Too much to do.
And so I would pick you up myself. I would tell you
to put your arms around me. Give your son a hug. Hold on.
I won't drop you. I promise. On the count of three.
And I would lift you gently up. And for a few seconds
with no music playing this is how we would dance.

Still Life with Goose in Mid-Flight

I pretend-shoot a lone goose
knowing I could never pull
a real trigger. That bird
belongs to that sky. Who am I
to say otherwise. I walk
alone and below wishing
I could fly. Even in water I have
trouble staying afloat.
This body of mine was never meant
for anything but this earth.

On My Morning Walk I Question What I See

All that I saw today along the road I asked if
it was my father. Each tree leaning over me,
each leaf, every stone I toed with my boot,
branches broken off in the night's hard rain,
even the clouds and birds flying beneath them:
Are you my father? Is this what you have become?

Fishing in the Rain with My Father

The storm blew in from the south
kicking up whitecaps out on the river.
I fished even after it started to rain.
Afraid of what? Getting a little wet?
I stood on the steel dock casting
a perch-colored Rapala into the wind.
The pike did not rise to take my bait.
It didn't matter one bit. I was happy
to be alive standing side by side
with my father dead thirty-eight days.

Under the Hood of My Father's '89 Lincoln Town Car

The battery is dead. At least it's easy to replace.
Even I can do that. And I do. The engine turns over
smooth, charged by what is brand new. I let it idle.
You could even say it purrs. I let the old gas run through.
My father would be proud. He taught his boy well, or at least
good enough, even though I always resisted those nights
with us leaning hunchbacked under the hood, the glow
of a single bare light bulb hanging between us, our shadows
stretched across the walls of the garage. His own heart
kept on, in spite of what else around it was breaking down.
Legs that no longer walked. Feet that could not hold him up.
Time for new tires, the mechanic might say. The nurses
showed us how to situate the pillows. To keep his feet raised.
You don't want his heels to blister. We did what we could
when we could. Which was always not enough. In the end,
for my mother, the open sores on his hips were the worst part
of watching him die. He let us go, back to our other lives,
before we could take him for one last drive around the island,
to see the river's other side. Now I ride alone. Or sometimes
with my son who says we need to get new rims for this bad boy.
But for now I leave it as it is. Low miles. Whitewalls facing out.

On What Would Have Been My Father's
Eighty-Seventh Birthday

I drive around the island looking for something.
For some sign that my father is here. The river's edge
is dotted with ducks—pintails and canvasbacks
diving for fish. The hawk at the top of a utility pole
gazes down looking for something too. Something to eat
I suspect. Two does and a young buck stare at me
as they try to figure out what to do with the metal fence
that is keeping them out. What little ice we see
on the river flows quietly on this windless evening,
the day's fading light also holding on as long as it can.
There is a dead tree floating out just beyond the red buoy.
Two seagulls are perched on it as it drifts out toward the lake.
They must be thinking: What is a tree doing in the water?
When night falls everything in this poem—the birds, the tree,
my father, the river—will remain what they are in the dark.

In the Twilight the Something That Is Always There

A single deer eating from the fruit of the mulberry tree.
The abundance that this doe found beneath her.
Dropped to the ground, green grass everywhere around.
Now speckled red and a deep rich, ripe purple.
Put there by the wind, or time passing, or the gods.
I watched her eat from inside the house with my mother
on her eighty-seventh birthday. And could not help but think
of my father, gone from us now these past fifteen months.
How the deer after it had eaten her fill knelt down in the shade.
And just sat there, looking at us who were looking at her.
Making a connection. Knowing that there was something there.

Where I'm From

The river. The birds. The trees.
The railroad tracks. Smokestack smoke.
The mud. Don't forget the rust.
The way it comes off on our fingers.
I could mix it with river water and mud
to make a paint to paint the landscape with.
But I don't paint. I wake up and I write. I fish.
What about the fish that I am from? I am a fish.
I am the river. The moon and the stars.
The river's winter ice. The summer's hum
of mosquitos and the cicada's song,
long-awaited after thirteen years underground.
The way they sing from their bodies.
They are singing to have sex and then die.
But enough about this common summer bug.
I am more from the song of birds and fish.
The tail slap of a carp. The cardinal's sharp trill
in the springtime as it also sings in its seeking
of a mate. The male's bold redness. The female
more modest in the way her feathers call for attention.
I am from those mornings when I go outside
to close my eyes and lift my face to listen.
The way as a child I used to go to church
to hear songs about death in a language I did not
speak and yet I felt the presence of the divine
cutting its way through the smell and smoke
of frankincense and the domed angels
stretched out above my head. These half-human
birds of God. How I wanted to run my hands
across them. So that I might better understand
the texture of wings, the language of leaving,
that other part inside us that is always seeking flight.

This Water, This Rock and Dirt, This River

I was made by water. This river.
This erosion of rock and dirt. This water
making mud. I have seen the fish
that do not rise from this river's murky
bottom. I have seen smokestacks
no longer making smoke. Have seen
the loon's webbed feet pushing against
this current, its diving head, wanting
not to be seen. I have heard these birds
calling across this water, a widow's
unveiled wailing to reach her husband,
this man standing alone in the fog in winter
waiting patiently on the river's other side.

On My Daughter's Twenty-Third Birthday

I am trying to remember twenty-three. I think
this was the year we moved out to Montana.
It didn't last. We lived, while we lived there,
in a cedar log cabin twenty miles outside
of Missoula on the edge of the Flathead
Indian Reservation and the Rattlesnake
Mountains. We had no choice. It was either
this or the shit-hole motor inn downtown
with the dented steel door that didn't lock.
Two women had lived in the cabin before us.
An ex-nun and a retired lieutenant from the Army.
Who knows what went sour there? The nun
took a wood-burning chisel to the heavy front
door and carved in the Ten Commandments.
She'd gone mad with either religion or jealousy.
We didn't stick around long enough to hear
the whole story. The two Harvard-educated
lawyers who now owned the cabin were looking
for company. They had a golden retriever
that shit in the house. The woman had eyes
that made me think of one of the Manson acolytes.
I woke up from a dream where she was standing
over our bed with a knife in her hand. Maybe
it wasn't a dream. Needless to say, we left
that morning. I don't regret a thing. Well maybe
Kalamazoo. We moved to Ann Arbor where
you were made. Born that December in Detroit.
And today you're twenty-three. The North Star's light
now entering our eyes has taken how many years
to get here? Too many. I'm glad you chose us.

What Is Always There Even When It Isn't

I don't know the names of most flowers.
Isn't it enough if I simply say yellow or blue?
It's spring. Rain is falling from the sky.
There are birds here too. They sing
no matter who might hear their songs.
If I said my name or told them that my father
is dying would their cadence alter?
When my father draws his last breath
will I be there to hear it? When I find
a feather on the ground I know only its silence.
When the petals on the flowers drop,
it's the green of the stem that's left standing, holding
what is left up. What remains constant is the dirt beneath us
which houses beauty always in what is otherwise dark.

Where What Was Still Alive Was Singing

I did not kiss my father after he died
but I did hold his hand. I touched him where
he was now mostly bone. It didn't take
long for his skin to grow cold. When the heart
no longer sends blood to warm the body.
I believe this is how it works. My father was dead
when his heart stopped and when his lips
no longer sputtered with breath. We watched
him slowly die. My mother couldn't get over
how fast she said it happened. He'd been dying
for years, I reminded her. She kissed him
on his mouth. Ran her fingers through his hair.
I walked down to the river. Where sunlight
lit the water. Where what was still alive
in my father followed with me. Where in a tree
I heard a bird singing. My father, his spirit,
hiding in the poplar branches blooming green.

We Looked for the Birds to Tell Us

We looked for the birds to tell us
where the fish were. Worked the boat
in above the schools of baitfish
upon which the birds and bigger fish
were feeding. Looking up to see
what we could not possibly see below.
Drifting down toward the birds and fish
all of them in that moment happy and eating.
Us about to eat soon too, a mix of pickerel and bass
that none of us would taste the difference.
The sky above was blue. The river a kind of blue too.
Eventually the hit was over, the birds and fish dissipated.
We ran the boat back upriver to the house
with no father inside it. Only a mother alone in her grief.
Sitting in the room where her husband died.
Looking out onto the evening's river. Thinking of what?
Feeling what none of us can ever completely know.
Gulping it down in silence. Saying no, shaking
her head with authority when she was asked to eat.

When the Loons Return to the River

When the loons return to the river
my father will be gone a year.
I don't want to hear them calling
from across these dark waters.
The sound they make makes me
want to dive headfirst underwater.
And hold my breath as long as I can.
Re-emerge days later. Downriver.
Under a bridge. Where the current
is especially swift. And the eddies
swirl around the concrete pilings.
And the undertow wears even
the strongest of swimmers down.

Bullhead

The bullhead I fished up from under the dock
had a wound on its side that made me think
of the bedsores my father had on his feet and hips
the last few days before he left us for good.
How upset my mother was when she saw them,
after priding herself on the fact she'd kept his body
so clean and so free of the skin breaking down.
We didn't think to turn him those final days
once he'd settled in for the sleep he would not
wake from, not even to eat or drink. He was leaving
this world for something and somewhere else.
The bullhead I set free after removing the barbed hook
with a pair of rusty pliers, careful not to get stuck
by its bony pectoral fin. It swam away into the dark river
waters but did not seem to have much fight left.
I turned and slowly walked back up from the dock
to say goodnight to my mother. The half-moon
had just started to rise. Half a man is how I now feel
when I enter that house where I'm the only father in it.

Almost Human

In my other lives I must have been a fish,
a bird, a tree, a stone, a river, or maybe
just a drop of water that is some small part
of a river. Why do we love what we love?
We see ourselves when a fish rises up
to break water or when a bird takes flight
or a tree in its many arms holds the sky.
The stone we pick up off the ground wants
to be held which makes it almost human.
The fish and birds, the trees and the river,
only want to be left alone. They pity us
our desire to be something that we aren't.

Sheepshead

The sheepshead floating on the surface
of the river was dead, its one eye staring up
at the sun. I rowed my little boat by it
just to make sure and to take a second look.
It was dead, its one eye staring at the sun.
Some things don't have to be looked at
more than once. When I was a boy I liked
to take a walking stick to all the things dead
on the side of the road. When I say things
what I mean to say is dogs, cats, deer, raccoons,
not to mention the crows and other birds
that like to eat other dead things on the side
of the road. When my father died I stood
off to the side of his bed to watch my mother
kiss his face and run her fingers through his hair.
Two hours later a woman with a stethoscope
listened to hear a heartbeat. There was none.
He was dead. It was official. This we already knew.
We dressed him one last time: a clean blue shirt.
A pair of underpants he hadn't worn in three years.
Gray sweats. I shaved his face. We washed his body
until it was as clean as a dead body needs to be.
The dead sheepshead that I rowed past on the river
had lost any hint of silver it once had. My father turned
to wood for the fire that would turn his bones to dust.
I carry him with me everywhere I go, everywhere I look.
I see him in the sky and in the river. The sheepshead
floating on its side, some part of it still impossibly alive.

What a Fish Is Not Supposed to See

Above the river the eagle appears
as I am leaving my father's house.
I am convinced this eagle is the father
of a good friend who left us in December.
The first time I saw him was the day
after he died, down at Pointe Mouillee,
perched at the top of an old maple,
its branches haggard, stripped of bark,
barren of leaves, dead for many years.
I looked up and watched him before turning
inland for a walk, and when I returned
he was gone. I felt as if we'd not said
our goodbyes. I've seen the eagle twice
since then. The first time he had a fish
hanging from his claws as he flew south
along the river toward the bridge before
turning inland for the woods and his nest.
Yesterday I saw him fish-less but fishing
the edges of the river's broken ice. I followed
his flight as long as I could, for as long
as he let me. I wanted to catch him in the act
of this taking, of soaring down from above,
the slow glide to the water below, leading up
to the open-clawed snatch. I wanted to watch
this caught fish ride this ascent, this view
into what a fish is not supposed to see,
of the river not above it but far below,
of death as it is seen heading for the trees,
flying in a way only a fish might dream,
wingless, its open mouth gulping cold air.
None of us in the end gets to choose
how we go, how we are taken, but to see
my own father carried through the sky
by an eagle above the river, I can't think
of a better way to say goodbye.

In a Poem He Might Praise the Birds

Nine months later and he is still writing
poems about the dying of his father.
Who was eighty-six when he died. Who had lived
a good life. Up until the last few years.
The years he lay in bed. And could not walk.
Let alone drive. When it got to be difficult
to talk. How the start of one sentence
would seek out the end of some other thought.
Imagine a river flowing up the side of a mountain.
Imagine a boulder that becomes a bird.
Maybe it was something similar to that.
He wishes he could offer up a better example
of how the mind took such great leaps. In a poem
he might praise how strangely the language moved
when spoken. How it was like a migrating bird flying
three thousand miles to reach the equator
without a map. He wishes he could equate
his father's broken speech to the flight patterns
of a specific bird. The black tern, for instance.
Whose nests are built on top of the water.
In the reeds. Out of bulrush stalks. In the shallows.
What happens when the surface waters get stirred up.
When summer storms bring with them heavy wakes.
When the eggs fall in, sink, and then disappear.
When the hatchlings, before they can fly,
get swallowed by bass and muskie and pike.

What I Still Feel Inside, or Some Other Darkness

When I was a child, I used to have to fight
the urge to throw rocks at birds. I often lost.
The rock would make its splash and the birds
would break into flight. Would scatter. Move
to a safer place, out of distance of my arm
strength. I would then be momentarily seized
by some other darkness, some other fascination
or death. I'd walk along the river looking for
dead fish, for bones, the feathers of birds
in mud. I'd toe them with a shoe, turn them over
with a stick, stick the stick into an eye socket.
I don't know if this made me a bad child.
Don't know if what I still feel inside makes me
a bad man. But even now, I find myself
wanting to disturb the peace of the geese
gathered in the sloughs down at Pointe Mouillee.
I see a rock on the levee or in the weeds.
And I reach down for it. I squeeze it hard.

Bones

I've been collecting the bones
of dead animals I find on my walks
through the marsh. The skull
of a muskrat so far is my favorite.
The teeth only slightly loose.
I carry these bones in my pockets.
Fish my fist down inside to feel them there.
I am a rich man, I say, as if each bone
is made of gold. Each hard piece
a kind of currency left behind
by those who have paid the price.

When Our Fathers Return to Us as Birds

Darkness this morning on what I know is
the shortest day of the year. Winter solstice.
Woke up to the news that a friend's father
has left us. *We lost the old man* is how
he put it to me. I had words to say back
but they're never the right ones. A handshake
or hug or hand on the shoulder fails us too.
Maybe what's best is to not say anything.
To let silence have its way with grief.
This friend and I had made plans earlier
in the week to get drinks tonight. Whiskey
around a backyard fire. We're sticking to it.
That's the kind of man my friend is. Like his father
always was. How he would have wanted it to be.
If there wasn't ice right now out on the river
we'd go fishing even though the boat has no lights.
The moon tonight will be mostly in darkness.
And the stars will be there too, as they always are,
as they always will be, when there's nothing more to say.

Not Able to Say It

New snow on this new morning
and I am happy to be able to say so.
My father on his island across the river
has reached the point where he is not able
to say it. He is not able to talk much
or walk at all. He can watch the snow
falling through the picture window
but can no longer hear it beneath his boots.
He must imagine what time has taken away.
He lives vicariously through his window.
There is the road with cars that slow down
to look at the river. There is the river and across the river
the smokestacks of the steel mill standing mute
against the gray sky. In the summer
I wheel him down to be closer to the water.
To see the buoy that blinks at night.
When a boat motors by he likes to guess the size.
A thirty-two-footer, he'll say. His eyes
are tape measures of exactness: I like the lines
of that one. He's pointing to a Sea Ray cutting upriver
though I can't help but think that in his mind
he is picturing someone he met in Korea
sixty-five years ago. I know my mother would say
she has forgiven him. He's suffered enough already.
Maybe that's what love looks like to the woman
in the pickup truck who always brakes to wave.
She sends my father greeting cards through the mail.
I am praying for you, she writes. What a beautiful view.

There Is Always Some Other Way to Say It

I don't know what to think when I see
the swans with their heads held underwater.
I imagine they are searching for food
but some part of me believes it's a game
they are playing to see how long they can hold
their breath. The way their white bodies are angled
up to face the sky like a kind of offering
or maybe just to dry that part of themselves out.
I am amazed at how long they can remain like that
without coming up for air, and so often without
a fish in their beaks. What some of us call a bill.
There is always some other way to say it.
When my father's breathing slowed we knew
it was only a matter of time. Minutes. Maybe an hour.
We watched, waited, hoped, prayed, for what?
He was dying. Departing. Passing on. Taking flight.
Then dead. Then dead. Then dead. Then dead.

The Swans Revisited

The swans seem to keep coming back
night after night. The darkness does not
cover up their whiteness. They remain
what they are, floating stars, regardless.

The Moth

The moth beats its wings harder than
I think it should have to. How it hovers near
the yellowing porch light. It is night still
this early in the morning. Stars and a moon
that every new day keeps lessening.
I wonder what I am and what this struggle
is trying to tell me. This insect that is not grace.
That crashes its dusty wings into this false
light that I know will someday burn out.
Everything does. First with a quiet flicker.
Then in its entirety, leaving us alone in the dark.

For My Mother

I try my best to imagine what it must be like
for my mother. Who misses my father most of all.
What it must be like for her to wake up at four
in the morning and to walk downstairs to an empty
room with my father no longer asleep in his bed.
Nothing for her to take care of any longer except for
the houseplants lining the floor along the window.
Outside the river flows as it always has and always will.
Some things don't change, even in death. The river
goes on and on, as do the rest of us. Meanwhile
my mother makes coffee and takes it over to the couch
where for three years she sat watching and taking care
of my father while the rest of us watched him die.
There was nothing any one of us could do to stop it.
Now he's dead. Now my mother sits alone in the quiet
waiting to join him. I try to imagine what that must be like.
But I can't do it. I want to live. I want to take over for my father.
There is a boat to tend to, trees to trim, a dog to be walked.

What Did I Know about Work

A year ago tonight, I imagine, I might have been
driving home late after a night teaching fiction
when a phone call from my mother asks me
if I can come over after work, that my father's bed
needs cleaning, that she is needing my help.
No problem, I tell her. I'll call you when I'm close.
And so I would. And did. Some nights my father
didn't even know how bad it was. He'd act surprised
to see me. Hey, Man, he'd say. How you doing?
As if his hands hadn't earlier been covered in shit.
As if his shit hadn't darkened beneath his nails.
I'm good, I'd always say, a lie I'd gotten good at.
Let's get you cleaned up. Some nights he was like
a cooing, cooperative infant, all nods, reaching out
with his body to be picked up. But other nights
it was like something primal in him had been awoken,
the way he'd lash out and gnash his teeth and bite.
It's okay, that's right, we're almost done, I'd lie again.
Those were nights I would rather not remember.
Eventually he would calm and the quiet of the night
outside would claim the darkness inside the house.
A few minutes later, I'd ask my mother if she was alright,
and she'd nod her own head and say she was fine,
I should go home now, I've had a long day at work,
go get some sleep. Work, I would think. What did I know
about work? I'd kiss both my mother and father
once on the forehead before turning toward the door.
You get some sleep, I'd say. And then I'd step outside,
into this other darkness, turning to face the river,
walking down to dip my hands into its dark waters,
looking away from where the real work was taking place.

Work Song

When a thing stops working take a hammer to it.
If the hammer doesn't do the job get a bigger hammer.
Hammer hard. This is how the gods get shit done.
This is how they break us down and keep us working.

Whatever It Was It Was an Honor, Call It a Privilege

Even the worst of it I want to hold onto.
Nights when my father would try to bite my hand.
When he would tell me to get the fuck out.
His bed and his body in the bed covered in shit.
Not because to say at least he was alive.
He was better off dead than to have to live like this.
But to come this close to whatever this was.
It was an honor. Call it a privilege. Not for my father.
Not for my mother who carried the weight of it.
I got to see what it is like to look down from above.
The gods in the end do little. No hands called on deck.
The river flows south before turning out into the lake.
The main river road on this island goes around in a circle.
I would often stay on it not wanting to cross the bridge home.
Some roads tell us dead end. Others say do not enter.
The night my father died I had to brake three times
to avoid hitting an animal crossing in front of me.
One was an opossum. One was a deer. The third thing
I could not tell what it was. It happened that quick.

What We Can't Get Rid Of

We cleaned out my father's shed today,
my mother and me. Got rid of things
we couldn't use, gave other stuff away:
generator, snowblower, lawn mower.
Patched a hole in the roof where I noticed
light was shining in. Where there's light
there is also rain. So much rain this spring.
And now, it's summer. Most days begin
with a gray skin of clouds. I don't mind
when it rains. I still like to take long walks
down to Pointe Mouillee with my dog.
I'm sore this morning after a six-mile hike
out onto Lake Erie with its freighters
filled with iron ore. On the tip of the Pointe
I am somewhere in between Toledo
and Detroit. I know there are better places
to be. I'm closer to Detroit, the city
where my parents were born and raised,
met in Delray's Southwestern High,
dated, went steady, fell in love, married.
The rest is history. Korean War. Three kids.
The midnight shift at Great Lakes Steel.
A house on an island. Sickness and death.
Everything else is a love story that's not mine
to tell. In my mother's words: "I devoted
my whole life to your father. He deserved it."

Guilty

My mother says she feels guilty
when she eats strawberries because
they were my father's favorite.
With sugar sprinkled on top. Says
the ice cream they both liked
also makes her cry as she sits
on the couch looking out at the river
watching the boats passing by.
She is passing the time. Waiting
for my father to walk back across
the river. To take her by the hand.
To whisper in her ear, "Forgive me."

In Greek the Word for Forgiveness

As a child God came to me as a foreign
language and the image of a beloved son
dead on the cross. What I heard was
an ancient music mixed with frankincense
and smoke. A man in a gold robe
wore his own hair like God's dead son.
The incantation of his name weighed heavy
on my head. Not what was said but how
the sorrow met with what I now understand
to be forgiveness. The widowed *yiayias* kneeling
near the altar weeping after so many years.
Not for the dead husbands that had been taken away
but for what was waiting for them upon the return:
a promise that when they were to be reunited
they would be young and beautiful in a way
that they never were in the first place.

Only the River Between Us

I don't know what to think or say when my mother says
that she is thinking about selling the house. The river
house. The house on the river. House of my father. A house
that in my father's eyes said he had finally made it.
Where my father walked until his legs could no longer hold him.
The house my father used to fall down in. The house
I would go to in the middle of a winter night to pick him up.
To put him back up into his bed in the living room with a view
of the river. His river. Our river. This muddy river. River
that sings us to it. River that pulls us in. Yes, the river
we would walk down to and fish. With my children. On the dock.
In the back of the boat. "Daddy, look, a fish." Fishing rods
bent with the pull and weight of the unseen parts of the river.
Fish scales shining when lifted up glistening in the summer's light.
Yes, we ate the fish, sometimes. Sometimes, though, we didn't.
If they were too small or not the right fish we would throw
them back. Tell them to come back when they were grown big.
Which of course these fish never did. Someone else fishing
caught them instead. And ate them. Or threw them back again.
Other fish came to where our lines were cast to take our bait.
Some of these fish we ate. Those children have left home now.
And the father of their father is dead. And in this house the mother
wakes up in the morning's four a.m. dark and looks around and sees
a house that is quiet and empty. This house that is hers alone now.
House made of fish bones, of broken birds' wings, of what once was.
Of my father. Our father. And only the river between us remains.

We Fish

I go with my son down to the river to fish,
even though catching fish is the least of it.
I bait his hooks with minnows and tell him
where to stand and what to watch for. I am
watching him fish but I am seeing myself
as a young boy waiting for that first bite.
I am waiting and watching and I am turning
around to say to my father, "I got a nibble."
When my father tells me to set the hook,
I pull back hard on the rod and reel in line.
There is no fish, the barbed hook hangs bare
of its bait. Try again, a voice says. Fishing
is about more than catching fish. Look
at all this water. Listen to the birds around us.
Is it me or is this my father? My son suddenly
is a man. We stand looking out on the river.
We fish until our buckets fill up with fish.

Fear and Death Which Is Different Than Fear of Death

The fear is that he will have nothing else to say.
And then what? Is this when the real grief
will begin to have its way? Will eat at his body
like a bedsore, or like fire, or like what beetles do
to whatever they find waiting for them in the dirt.
The way a small child must eat what is given.
As long as he was able to say something about it,
his father was in some strange and miraculous way
still alive. If he has no more to say, won't this be
a kind of second death? *My father. My father. My father.*
He writes. In this way language is the only living thing
between him and death. What else is there in the end?
What better reason to keep on writing and pushing back
against time and death with the heart in his body still singing.

I Am Afraid I Am Going to Forget

Not his face. Not the purple blisters on his feet.
Not the yellow tube or the bag for urine that hung
from the railing of his bed. But the little things.
Like when he offered me his hand to shake it.
Or the way his upper lip always disappeared
when he smiled for pictures. All the times
he walked the dog. The day he helped change
the doorknob in our brownstone in Detroit.
Every poem I write is not so I can get distance.
I am wanting to remember to remain close.
How his voice always trembled giving toasts.
The bags under his eyes growing red and puffy.
I could go on and on, the forces of memory.
The way his legs folded in up close to his chest
like a flower closing against a moonlit night.
How at the end he turned his face to look away
from the river. So that we might see beyond
our father in his dying. What was happening
in the darkness on the river's other side.

On the Other Side of the River

What happens on the other side of the river
stays on the other side of the river. Just as when
the dead are taken away they do not return
looking as they once did. There are birds
and fish both of which sometimes wash ashore
no longer able to fly or swim. The dead
in their most silent form, with no song other
than what words we might say of them.
I have no more songs other than this.
These hands that reach down into the mud
to hold them one last time, before I put them back
where I found them, and then walk away.
Making a humming sound only I can hear.

So Much of What We No Longer Want

So much of what we no longer want
ends up in the river. Lately I've been noticing
an abundance of old tires from cars.
A tractor tire too. Big enough for a child
to crawl up inside. The river water
not deep enough to cover the rubber up
and so it is only half submerged.
In the summer, turtles like to sit there
in the sun until they notice someone is watching.
At which point they will dive and disappear
into the murky shallows. I don't mean to disturb them.
But I know that I do in the same way I know
that one day I won't be taking long walks along
this marsh where the river widens out into the lake.
The currents that keep pushing things downriver.
The wind, when it shifts, sometimes moves the water
in new directions. Sometimes small boats end up
getting blown out to waters bigger than what
they can take. Sometimes these boats take on water
and sink. Bodies that never get found. Or when they do
they look nothing like the faces in the photographs
taped to light poles and trees. It takes years for rubber
to break down. One summer a junkyard filled with old tires
caught fire and kept burning for three weeks. Smoke
could be seen for over twenty miles. There was this smell
you knew could only be human. Even the fires
of the mills rising up from the chemical mud along the river
eventually burn out. McLouth Steel. Great Lakes Steel.
Zug Island. The river takes whatever it is given. Sometimes
it takes and takes some more and does not give it back.

Dead Man's Point

On a walk with four dogs out to Dead Man's Point
we do our best not to talk about death. We fail.
What is it about the water that brings us always back
to how things end? What's more mysterious
are the middle parts when we are far enough away
to think there is still more time in front of us than what
we have left behind. We walked until the evening
grew in all around us on a day that to begin with had little
light pushing through the winter sky. The dogs ran off
ahead of us in their search for other animals already dead.
Only one dog was more interested in flushing out
from the tall marsh grasses that which was still alive.
She ended up back at the car before us and was there waiting
in the dark and did a little circle dance when she saw us.
Which was not like her. Something's not right with Rio,
you said. She looks like she might be in heat, I pointed out.
Who knows what it could be? Rio danced for us again.
Making more circles in the mud with the darkness getting darker
as we watched her and listened to the quiet of no more words
about death and the birds hidden in the silence around us.

On the River with Time Being What It Is

They are tearing the mill down to mud.
Taking the black steel to its bones.
Yesterday they punched out the windows,
green glass blocking the view inside.
So now from the road you can see through
across the river. To the river's other side.
And the house where my mother lives.
House where my father died looking out
at the water. At the mill like a freighter
run aground and rusting. No longer making
fire and steel. Silent in the river's dark.
What my father would think I don't know.
I think he would think it's a good thing.
But also that some part of him would miss it.
We get used to what is always visible.
The way my father in his bed unable to walk
made him more alive. Or at least present.
It was what I knew I would always find
waiting when I walked in through the door.
He was there no matter the time of day.
Now from the same window he looked out
I watch the yellow excavators bending metal.
Soon there will be nothing left. Only the river
that can be trusted to flow out to the lake.
Except when a strong wind out of the south
blows it back to its source. Back toward the city
where my father was born. Where he'd drive
lost in the dark trying to find his way back home.
The way I drive by girded beams and smokestacks
that hold up the sky. At least for the time being.

Deadwood

The firewood behind my father's shed
is so old it's rotted down to mostly sawdust.
I want to burn up what I can but the wasps
who've made a nest out of all the dead wood
have other ideas. One of them stings me
in the armpit. I tell my mother to go inside,
that we'll take care of this later. She wants
to get rid of what she can while she still can
be of use. She can bend down to pick up
a stick off the ground as if she isn't eighty-six.
I'm only fifty-two but the twig sometimes wins
the battle between should I or shouldn't I
and it gets to stay another night out of the pit
of my backyard bonfire. I never imagined
I'd watch my father get turned into ashes
but I was there when the man in a blue
work shirt with his name patched above his heart
rolled my father's body into that furnace,
a button pushed to light those final flames.
I wanted to look but there was nothing to see,
nothing but a cardboard box with my father's name
written on it, all of it about to go up in smoke.

Wood, Wings, Bones

I prefer the trees in winter when the wood
is more apparent. Just south of Gibraltar Road
there is an eagle's nest visible even
through all the leafy green. It is the season
of newness everywhere, when the old houses
in need of paint look even more barren and beautiful.
When my wife and I saw the white pelicans
they flew in a four-bird formation and hovered
in the blue sky reminding us of a child's kite.
Out on Vermet Bay the rest of the flock remained
distant and elusive, another hour-long walk out
onto the dike. We were temporarily gifted by our four,
even though they soon left us to join the others.
The Great Blue Heron with a fish in its beak breaking
into flight as we were leaving was as miraculous
as if a fifty-year-old maple tree had sprouted wings.
As if the earth itself was lifting us into the sky.
As if we too had flown, our bones suddenly hollow.

Tell That to Our Fathers, or On the Eve of My Fifty-Third Birthday, Pointe Mouillee, 2019

What set the bald eagle apart from the other birds
we saw yesterday down at the marsh was the grandness
of its wings. Who are we to say that this magnificent bird
wasn't one of our fathers? It flew by us on its way
to somewhere else. I want to say that it turned its head
to look at us for a brief moment but that would be a fiction.
The eagle cut back against the wind in search of what: a tree,
another bird or fish to eat, or maybe something else
we can know nothing about. The dogs walked ahead of us
on the levee unaware of what we were maybe thinking.
Snow was blowing in off the lake. In the distance the lighthouse
readied itself to begin its nightly blinking. Across the river
in Canada the windmills were turning. Today I turn another year
older. Fifty-three. Can you believe it? Where I feel it most
is in my knees. Tell that to our fathers, wings spread in the sky.

Briefly It Might Have Even Flown

We walk along the dirt and gravel dike that runs
through the marsh with our dog Moonshine between us.
To our left the lake stretching out for Ontario.
Off to our right the low-water sloughs recently thawed.
Two swans fly overhead with their long necks pointed toward Ohio.
Later, we come upon a dead duck not yet eaten by a coyote.
I turn it over with my boot and toe it down the bank.
Where it lands with its face up to the sky. A fresh kill, I say.
Something will come along and make use of it, I think. For now
it lives again here in this poem. A kind of preservation.
Had I picked it up with my hands and thrown it, briefly it might have
even flown. A momentary resurrection. Power beyond our own.

ACKNOWLEDGMENTS

The author wishes to acknowledge the editors of the following publications where certain of these poems were first published:

Bennington Review: "More Birds Than I Know What to Do With" and "What I Still Feel Inside, or Some Other Darkness"
Kenyon Review: "What My Father Did Not Have to Say" and "What I Know Is Not My Father"
Respect: The Poetry of Detroit Music: "On Turning Fifty-Two"
Unsaid: "Slow Dance with My Father with No Music," "This Water, This Rock and Dirt, This River," "Practice," "Brothers and Fathers and Sons," "South of White Rock, Lake Huron, July, 1979," "There Is Singing," "Walking Out Alone onto the February River," "What Was Never His to Begin With," "Under the Hood of My Father's '89 Lincoln Town Car," "Where I'm From," "On My Daughter's Twenty-Third Birthday," "When Our Fathers Return to Us as Birds," "There Is Always Some Other Way to Say It"

Thanks too to early readers of these poems, most notably Dan Wickett and Russell Thorburn who encouraged him to keep writing "the book you've been waiting your whole life to write."

And Jeff and Greg Mans for showing him the marsh.

He also wishes to thank his sister Sue for first putting the bird in his mouth. And Dana and Markus and George for being a part of this journey.

And Helena and Sol for making him a father.

And Rebecca for holding him up.

And to Annie Martin and everyone at Wayne State University Press for bringing this book back home.

ABOUT THE AUTHOR

Peter Markus is the author of six books of fiction, including *The Fish and the Not Fish*, which was named a Michigan Notable Book in 2015, and coeditor with Terry Blackhawk of *To Light a Fire: 20 Years with the Inside-Out Literary Arts Project* (Wayne State University Press, 2015). Markus is the senior writer with InsideOut Literary Arts and is on the faculty at Oakland University, where he teaches creative writing. In 2012, he received a Kresge Arts in Detroit fellowship in Literary Arts.